THE AUTHORITY GUIDE TO WRITING & IMPLEMENTING A MARKETING PLAN

A step-by-step manual to make you a smarter marketer and maximise your business profits

AMBROSE & JO BLOWFIELD

The Authority Guide to Writing and Implementing a Marketing Plan
A step-by-step manual to make you a smarter marketer and maximise your business profits
© Ambrose and Jo Blowfield

ISBN 978-1-909116-90-0
eISBN 978-1-909116-91-7

Published in 2017 by Authority Guides
authorityguides.co.uk

The right of Ambrose and Jo Blowfield to be identified as the authors of this work has been asserted by them in accordance with the Copyright, Designs and Patents Act 1988.

A CIP record of this book is available from the British Library.

All rights reserved. No part of this book may be reproduced, stored in a retrieval system, or transmitted in any form or by any means, electronic, mechanical, photocopying, recording or otherwise, without the prior written permission of the publisher.

No responsibility for loss occasioned to any person acting or refraining from action as a result of any material in this publication can be accepted by the author or publisher.

Thank you Jacqui Hunt for your endless love, belief and support and Ian Blowfield for your investment into my education to help me do what I now do.

Thank you William and Juanita Pratt, for all your help, love and support over the many years of us growing our business and family.

And to our daughters, Arabella and Asia-Rose, you are the reason we do the late nights, worldwide travel and crazy hours. Keep believing that everything is possible. You are our inspiration.

The value of an idea lies in the using of it.

Thomas Edison
serial inventor and master marketer

Contents

Introduction	vii
1. The changing world of business	1
2. Our journey	5
3. The Profit Pillars of Marketing™	11
4. Marketing proposition: external analysis	19
5. Marketing proposition: internal analysis	25
6. Marketing communication: non-digital	37
7. Marketing communication: digital	51
8. Implementing your plan	65
Conclusion	69
The TMC Authority Guide Marketing Plan Template™	71
About the authors	75
Who is THE Marketing Company?	77

Theory is splendid but until put into practice, it is valueless.

James Cash Penney
founder of J C Penney

Introduction

Whether you are established in business, in a start-up business or looking to start a business, congratulations on choosing to invest in your marketing knowledge in order to create the right future for your business. By purchasing this book you are already ahead of most, and by implementing the proven steps in this book you will likely succeed more than ever in your chosen industry.

Traditionally quoted statistics in the UK, the US and elsewhere suggest that only 10 per cent or 20 per cent of small to medium enterprises (SMEs) reach their fifth birthday, and only 4 per cent reach their tenth. Thankfully, more recent research by statisticbrain.com states that 45 per cent of American SMEs reach five years old and 29 per cent make it to ten. This is in line with New Zealand's Department of Statistics that claims that 66 per cent of SMEs make it to the age of four. What's more important to note however is that statisticbrain.com also found that 46 per cent of start-ups failed due to incompetence. Of the seven stated areas of incompetence, three were marketing-related. A further 11 per cent of new businesses failed due to lack of experience, with one key area being wasting advertising budget. As Michael Gerber beautifully explains in *The E-Myth Revisited*, being an experienced technician in your field does not guarantee you business success.

Statistics state that half of SMEs do have a marketing and/or business plan. However, in our work around the world we have found that number to be very misleading. Over 75 per cent of businesses we meet don't actively follow a plan each week or each month. While many have plans, most of them have been gathering dust after it was used to convince a bank or business partner to support the business concept. As a result a number of things happen:

- Many businesses waste time second-guessing and debating their marketing decisions.
- Some don't fully commit to their decisions, so even when they make a right decision they may miss results by stopping too soon (there is usually a time lag in marketing between taking action and achieving results).
- Some businesses miss out on opportunities by not planning to do the right things (busy people often make quick decisions that are not always the right decisions).
- Many waste money on the wrong decisions and/or miss out on opportunities by not making decisions at all.

The outcome of this is often lower profits, unproductive time, team demoralisation and ultimately a long-term threat to business survival. Regardless of which business failure statistics you believe, what is certain is that most of the world's most respected companies – in any industry, large and small – are marketing driven.

Take a moment to prove this: write down 5–10 companies you believe to be really successful and ask yourself: how strong you think they are in their marketing compared to others in their industry? You see, marketing is at the start of the entire business cycle: it defines what you sell, to whom and whether you have any customers at all for your operations, admin, accounts and other divisions to serve.

Marketing is changing

The old approach to marketing was limited to only a few main communication options: TV, radio, newspapers, magazines and billboards. As in any basic supply and demand relationship, these limited options and growing demand drove the cost up. The outcome was that the larger businesses could invest more and it became an advantage that only larger companies could truly win, people like Proctor & Gamble, Coca-Cola and McDonald's.

Today, however, the world of business is changing – the success stories are no longer coming from the old economies of scale, the present and the future belongs to economies of speed: the Snapchats, the Ubers, the local specialists of the world. This is what all SMEs have in common: they can make fast decisions, take quick action and measure quickly to improve. The future belongs to those that leverage these economies of speed.

The new trend is that SMEs can rival larger companies for customer loyalty (craft beer producers being a prime example). The globally-connected nature of business means that people can easily buy directly and indirectly from SMEs worldwide, regardless of their location. Meanwhile people can start businesses more easily, and as the traditional industrialised workforce model moves into decline, the number of microbusinesses will grow exponentially. *All* those businesses have one need in common: the need to understand marketing in order to have customers.

When we committed to THE Marketing Company full time in 2005, we found ourselves needing to market to a local economy that barely understood marketing nor felt they needed it. We would try things that did work and we would try things that didn't work. An early breakthrough came when we set ourselves really ambitious goals, we wrote down our tactics to achieve them, and we didn't take the knockbacks as a sign to stop trying. We stopped thinking of our business as a local regional marketing consultancy and chose to become a nationwide marketing and sales training business. Since that day we have been privileged to train over 6,000 businesses in over 12 countries across three continents, helping them to make millions in extra sales. This book contains many of the lessons we've learnt along the way – both first hand and through our customers. We wish to thank them sincerely for allowing us to share their stories and lessons.

The great news is that all the things we have found to make people successful through their marketing are learnable, measurable and repeatable. If you want to build a sustainable, long-term, profitable business, using proven marketing techniques, then this is the book for you, regardless of whether you're new to business or fully established.

By reading, implementing and re-reading this *Authority Guide* you will achieve greater results from your marketing, increased profit margins, more fun at work, more predictable sales flow, greater motivation, higher confidence levels and more control of your business's future.

You will learn how marketing has changed and yet stayed the same: how to get your marketing proposition (offering) right, what traditional marketing tactics you should still use and what digital tactics you should also be using to grow your business. Better still, you will learn how to take action, complete a marketing plan and implement that plan to maximise your business success. Be aware: once you gain an appreciation for marketing and the results it produces, you may even end up liking this critical area of business!

1. The changing world of business

As you will have realised, the nature of business has changed, as has the nature of marketing. To understand marketing a couple of decades ago you probably had to attend multiple years of higher learning followed by several years working in a full-time marketing role, or an advertising agency, or working in a truly marketing-driven business. These days you can, and should, acquire marketing know-how on a weekly basis and in smaller bite-sized pieces. By applying *and* measuring those techniques you can learn quickly while growing your business.

Even measuring your marketing, once the competitive advantage of large organisations, is now easier for SMEs than it has ever been. With a little planning and effort you can easily measure over 80 per cent of your marketing activities and results, allowing you to make changes more easily and implement new actions quickly.

When the marketing world was dominated by advertising, a standard commitment for any business was for a 6- or, more likely, 12-month contract. This meant that if you made the wrong decision at the start of a year, there was little you could do except write the money off or, worse still, 'hope' for a better outcome. We believe that there are times in your life for hope, but the marketing of your business is *not* one of those times!

1. The changing world of business

For those of you about to launch a new business or new division, or even those in that start-up phase, you can research the market and learn about your chosen industry more easily and quickly than ever before – using websites, industry forums and social media. Never before in human economic history has there been a better time to launch a new business, a new product or service, or a new division.

As stated, many businesses do not survive their first five years, while many more stagnate long term. Too many businesses, despite having seen first hand the benefits of planning parts of their business or personal lives, get to a point where they stop planning – drifting towards mediocrity, following the path of wholly reactive behaviour, ending in disappointing results.

Clearly a more proactive approach is needed by SME business owners and soon-to-be start-up entrepreneurs. Surely there is a way to follow a proven path to business knowledge and success, a way to combine the more traditional proven marketing tactics with the dynamic and ever-changing new marketing tools?

We passionately believe that in this new world of social media, mobile marketing and online marketing, the winning businesses will be those that learn, apply, review and tweak their ongoing marketing. The losers will be those businesses where the owners or managers don't plan, don't measure and don't implement.

We're keen to share that we're still following the same methodologies as we've always done: we still read, we still attend events, we still network to learn from others in business and we still make ourselves do uncomfortable things to keep us growing – like writing a book! Recently, to stay up to date in digital marketing we both ended up listening to half an hour of podcasts on digital marketing per day at 1.5 times speed, simply to get through the content more quickly!

This is not a guide for dummies – as we know from the thousands of people we've worked with in business, small to medium business owners and managers are not dummies, they're incredibly strong technically in what they do, it's just that many of them haven't had the time to understand marketing yet. This *Authority Guide* is a practical step-by-step manual that you can come back to again and again for reference. If you put it away for 12 months, simply bring it out to rewrite your marketing plan again. But keep in mind that some aspects of marketing will have changed by then, especially in the digital marketing space. Best SME practice is to rewrite your marketing plan annually. Despite marketing being a wide topic, based on over a decade of working with thousands of SMEs around the globe, we have condensed what you really need to know to grow your business into these short pages. Use the scaled down marketing plan template guide at the back of this book to create your plan, or better still visit THEmarketingcompany.com (search: Authority Guide) for a free online template to save you even more time when implementing. It will be easier to complete your marketing plan as you go through this book, the action points are at the end of each chapter to guide you.

The winners in life think constantly in terms of I can, I will and I am. Losers, on the other hand, concentrate their waking thoughts on what they should have or would have done, or what they can't do.

Denis Waitley
author of *The Psychology of Winning*

2. Our journey

Growing our business has been challenging, fun, overwhelming, exhilarating, scary and wonderful and we're sure you have experienced this too. As many of you will have learned in your business or personal lives, having a clear motivation for taking action is often a key ingredient to you *doing* something. For us that motivation came from having our home and investment property mortgaged fully, having our first child and deciding that in order to spend more time together we needed to work together.

So we read every business book that people we trusted recommended to us, we attended paid and free talks, we listened to business and personal development books on CDs, we networked with successful people to ask them questions about how they achieved success and we made ourselves speak publicly in front of audiences (despite our nerves). Through doing all these things, we steadily built our confidence, we accelerated our business and we developed the habit of ongoing learning and implementation.

Our first two challenges were self-inflicted. The first came from starting the business with only NZ$1,500 (then about £500 or US$1,000), without even pre-negotiating access to more bank

2. Our journey

funds if required. The second came from not knowing that in order to get paid in month two we needed to invoice people in the first month! Four months later and our core values were tested by our first regular monthly client who refused to take the advice we gave them. Our purpose in business has always been to make a positive difference. The client chose to advertise their business a certain way, a way that we knew would generate zero results, and despite our advice they spent their hard-earned profits anyway, achieving zero results. We measured the results with them and suggested not to repeat the mistake again, taking time to explain why it would be another waste of money. They chose to advertise again, this time mentioning that their family loved seeing them advertise as it made them look successful. This was our first experience of ego-based marketing: choosing to advertise for personal pride and not for business gain. Having politely, awkwardly – and financially painfully for us as a young business – let the client go for choosing to waste money, we walked away with two important lessons that we can now share:

- *Never* compromise on your beliefs or values, your business success will come without the need to change who you are or how you choose to act.
- *Never* put your own ego above the business, you serve your business and by doing so correctly it, in turn, will serve you.

Having grown the business locally, we decided to open another office with a full-time employee, only to be hit with the tail end of the Global Financial Crisis. Which two things did businesses, large and small, cut back on in recession? Yes, marketing and training! So as a sales and marketing training company we were cut back on both sides, watching our number of enquiries AND our conversion rate of enquiries to sales drop by over 65 per cent! For example, the results from talks we delivered around the country (an example of public relations) changed from 30 attendees leading to 3 sales of our 12-month sales programme, to fewer than 1 sale per event! We did everything good marketers do – we looked at our 4 Ps of Marketing. We changed the Product offering to our marketing boot camp (so it became a two-day commitment not 12 months), we changed the Price by doing this (the boot camp was ¼ of the investment of our 12-month programme), we changed the Place by delivering in new towns and new venues (for our promotional talks and for our marketing boot camp), we even changed the person used to Promote the event and the pitch itself! Despite small changes, the trend was the same: if we really wanted to make up for a drop of 65 per cent, we'd have to treble our marketing activities in the short term to make up for the market change. The lesson we learned was that it's only by measuring your marketing activities and results that you can truly commit to significant change. We also had our resolve tested: both refusing to give up on the dream of business ownership by resisting offers of full-time employment elsewhere.

While the 18 months of recession we faced were tough, the lessons we learned were priceless and they have led us to grow an international training business and do what we love in life: helping SME businesses make more money through improving their sales and marketing skills, confidence and knowledge. Now we are thrilled to deliver both face-to-face and online training right around the world, helping to change the world one business at a time.

We have seen literally hundreds of our clients double their turnover, their net profits and their impact on the world. We've watched in awe as some clients have gone from start-up to million-dollar businesses in a couple of years, and medium-sized ones have broken through their respective glass ceilings in their industries. For over a decade we have been humbled by the stories and feedback people have shared with us.

The key is to take action

Having read this book there are a number of hurdles you'll likely have to overcome. Ideally you'll complete your marketing plan as you read through this book – which means you'll overcome hurdle number one: completing your marketing plan. It may feel like a big task, especially if you've never written a marketing plan before. You may not trust in your marketing knowledge so you may face a challenge with your confidence. You may not have someone to support you and hold you to account.

We'll deal with each hurdle in turn, starting with completing your marketing plan. If you've read this book, you have the foundation knowledge to complete your plan. Using our simple online template combined with the book, you can probably complete your plan in a matter of hours. You must start by blocking out time in your calendar: this is likely to be after hours or in your free time. If marketing isn't your first love in business, we recommend no more than 90-minute blocks of time, giving yourself a mini-reward after every block of time. If you lack marketing confidence, think back over your career or your personal life: *everything* you've ever become confident at you needed to do for the first time at some stage. You likely do something confidently every day, such as using a software programme, analysing a client problem, or fixing an issue, that didn't come naturally at first. Accountability is important. If you don't have a mentor, a coach or someone to hold you to account to make you complete your marketing plan using this *Authority Guide*, ask for someone right now. That way you'll be held to account by them to finish this book and finish your marketing plan! Stop reading and do it now! Don't be afraid to hold someone else in business to account in their marketing in order that they ensure you implement your plan. Finally, a story that keeps many of our clients motivated: if your competitor were a fly on the wall right now observing you, what would they rather see you do: do nothing and stay the same, or commit to change and take action towards a more successful future? Having found the answer, you simply need to do the opposite to what your competitor wants!

> If you learn from defeat, you haven't really lost.

Zig Ziglar
sales guru

3. The Profit Pillars of Marketing™

A particular challenge for SMEs is that due to the limited resources of money they often need to invest time instead of cash into their marketing. The challenge is that it's so easy to get drawn into other duties that we end up becoming sporadic with our marketing efforts. Without a timeline plan our sporadic efforts lead to peaks and troughs of activity which in turn lead to peaks and troughs in sales results.

> **Top tip**
>
> Learning to prioritise your time is critical. If you've not read *The 7 Habits of Highly Effective People* by Stephen Covey, we highly encourage you to do so. As you can see from the table below, there are four types of tasks: tasks are either urgent or not urgent, important or not important. By combining these definitions you get four types of task. Most people spend the majority of their lives at work in Quadrant One: doing things that are both urgent and important. They wait until the last minute to get things done, sometimes proud of how they 'saved the day' and sometimes addicted to the adrenaline rush of living day to day in mild panic. The problem with living in Quadrant One is that tasks keep sliding across from Quadrant Two as time passes. Hence the more

time you spend in Quadrant One, the more you stay stuck in Quadrant One. Highly effective people do things differently. They prioritise tasks based on importance rather than urgency, plus they schedule important tasks to be completed *before* they become urgent: they focus on Quadrant Two tasks. Reading this book and planning the next 12 months of your marketing is an example of a proactive Quadrant Two task, so well done in becoming more effective.

Figure 1 Stephen Covey's Time Management Matrix

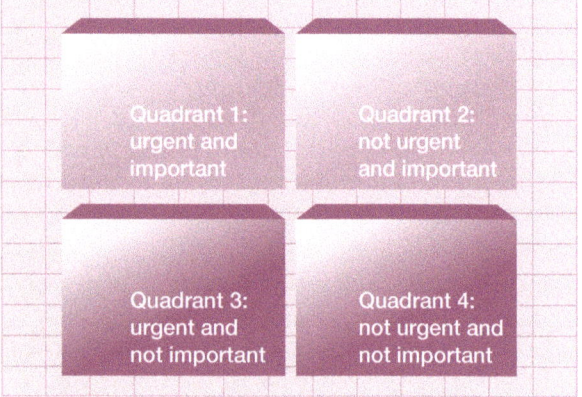

The Profit Pillars of Marketing™ are about purpose and outcomes. Although we measure sales, the real heart or purpose of a business is profit. In fact one of the only company laws you must abide by in most countries is the need to trade solvently, i.e. make a profit. The profit pillars will help you to know how to do that. We're not saying that a drive for profits should surpass other goals such as giving, helping others or making a difference in the world – simply that it's your duty to be profitable, plus it's a whole lot more fun and easy to give once you have been profitable in the first place.

There are five things you can achieve from your marketing in order to maximise profits. These make up The Profit Pillars of Marketing™:

1. You can increase your number of customers.
2. You can increase how much they spend each time.
3. You can increase your profit margin (how much money you keep).
4. You can increase the number of customers that come back as repeat purchasers.
5. You can increase how much people refer others to you.

Figure 2 The Profit Pillars of Marketing™

[Figure: Five pillars labelled "Customer numbers", "Speed per purchase", "Profit per purchase", "Repeat purchases", "Referrals" supporting a pediment labelled "Profit", standing on a base of "Marketing communication" above "Marketing proposition".]

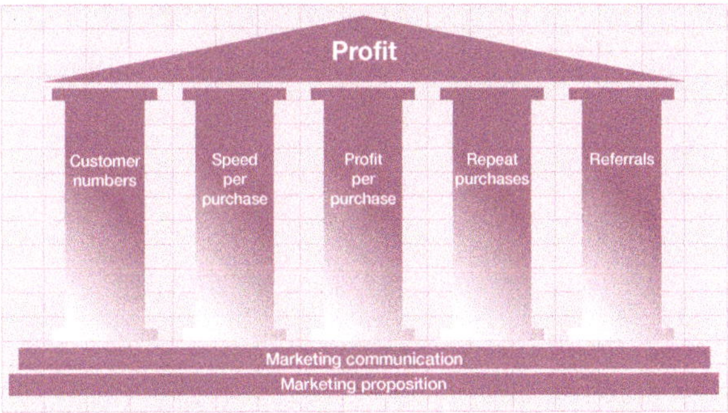

All of the marketing that you do needs to tactically help with one or more of the five pillars. If you can't work out which one of the pillars a new campaign or tactic should help, don't do it until you can. Pillars one and five focus on new customer acquisition. Pillar four focuses on customer retention. Pillars two and three

> **For example**
>
> 1. You can attract more customers through online advertising or trade shows.
>
> 2. You can increase how much they spend through bundling products together (like McDonald's 'meals') or by training your sales team to up-sell more.
>
> 3. You can increase your profit margins through increasing your prices or having better packaging to raise brand perception.
>
> 4. You can increase repeat purchasers through e-blasts/e-shots or client gifts.

focus on both. You'll notice one item that isn't on that list is 'getting your name out there': this is an outdated view on marketing still used by lazy salespeople selling advertising space.

Now let's look at the profit implications. As you can see in the first table, Company A has 1,000 customers, each spending £1,000 each, of which there's a 50 per cent gross profit margin, while each customer buys twice per year, and two in every five customers refer a new customer to Company A. At the end of the year Company A makes £1,400,000 in gross profit.

Now to Company B – who read this book, completed and then implemented their marketing plan! As a result they got slightly better at each of the five Profit Pillars of Marketing™ (10 per cent better at each to keep the maths simple). They have 1,100 customers, each spending £1,100 each, of which there's a 55 per cent gross profit margin, while each customer buys 2.2 times per year and just over half their customers refer a new customer to Company B. At the end of the year Company B makes a massive £2,254,714 in gross profit!

Not only does Company B make higher profits, they likely have more fun in doing so. Of critical importance is that Company B didn't have to do a huge amount more work than Company A: to cope with an extra 100 customers per year didn't require a larger team or building, to increase the client spend and profit margins likely didn't require a huge investment, nor did coping with more repeat purchases or referrals. Company B simply got slightly smarter at The Profit Pillars of Marketing™. We want you to become Company B from this example.

We appreciate that if you are part of a franchise group, you may have a fixed amount of how much you could sell a product for (Pillar two). Or it may be a challenge for you to alter profit margins (Pillar three). All that means is that you must focus on the other pillars even more.

> **Take action now**
>
> As best as you can, thinking over the past 12 months, try filling in the left-hand side of the table.
>
> Then consider whether you can realistically improve in all five Profit Pillars of Marketing™.
>
> Calculate how much gross profit you could make by improving a little in as many of the five Pillars as possible.

Table 1 Comparison of Company A and Company B and use of the five Profit Pillars of Marketing™

Area	Company A	Company B
Number of customers	1,000	1,100
Average spend/purchase	1,000	1,100
Average profit per purchase (as a decimal)	0.5 (i.e. 50%)	0.55 (i.e. 55%)
Number of purchases per year (or other chosen time period)	2	2.2
Number of referrals per customer (as a decimal)	1.4 (meaning 2 in every 5 customers refer someone else)	1.54 (meaning just over half the customers refer someone else)
Total gross profit	1,400,000	2,254,714

Table 2 Your business and the five Profit Pillars of Marketing™

Area	Your business now (or past 12 months)	Your business in the next 12 months
Number of customers		
Average spend/ purchase		
Average profit per purchase (as a decimal)		
Number of purchases per year (or other chosen time period)		
Number of referrals per customer		
Total gross profit		

Just like building a house, you need all aspects of your marketing to be done right. There are two sides of marketing: marketing proposition and marketing communication. In turn, each of those parts has two sections: for the proposition external analysis and internal analysis are required, while for communication there are non-digital and digital communication options. It is by focusing on all four of these areas, that you can drive business success through your marketing.

Put simply: marketing proposition means 'who you are' 'what you do' and 'how you do it'. Marketing communication means 'how you tell the world what your marketing proposition is'.

This book focuses more on marketing communication for one simple reason: you likely know who you are or you wouldn't be reading this book. You typically know what it is that you do (or intend to do) and you probably know where you'll sit in the market place already. You're more likely looking for ways to affordably and successfully communicate your message better in order to generate more sales and profits.

4. Marketing proposition: external analysis

You could, and some do, spend months on the external analysis phase. The major risk to an SME of this is paralysis by analysis. Business moves pretty fast: you must take action. While we'd love you to spend more time researching the market, especially to determine that there is a market to serve, this chapter is all about the critical areas you must cover and none of the clutter you may not have to.

Key points in this chapter:

- Target market
- Market analysis
- O and T of SWOT analysis
- Competitor analysis

Target market

As the old adage states: 'If you try to be all things to all people, you'll end up being nothing to no one.'

It is important therefore, to choose who your target market is, to avoid casting your net too wide. In 2014, *Fortune Magazine* published CB Insights results that the number one cause of business failure for start-ups was from the lack of market need, and this reason was part of the reason for a huge 42 per cent of start-up failures. Getting clear on who you serve and whether they're interested is vital to your success.

Take a minute from the whirlwind of business and life to ask yourself: 'If I could choose only 3–5 different groups of businesses to serve (if you sell B2B) or groups of individuals to serve (if you sell B2C), who do I want to serve most?' The answers will likely come from a number of factors, some personal and some commercial. For example: 'We want to work with manufacturing companies in the UK, within 100 miles of Birmingham, who have 200–500 staff but no more, and are over 20 years old.' Once you choose the target markets to go after, and having checked that such a market actually exists and is large enough to support your business goals, you set up your marketing to target these markets above all else. If you happen to pick up other customers from other markets, you welcome it, the key is to focus over 80 per cent of your marketing efforts towards your target markets.

Market analysis

You can go really deep into this area of analysis. For now, there are some critical questions you must ask yourself about the target markets you serve. One question to ask is about what's happening in their world, i.e. 'What changes are expected in each of my target markets in the next 12 months or more?'

The second question to ask is: 'What factors are each of my target markets affected by?' For example, an import and distribution business will be directly impacted by exchange rates.

Next up is: 'How often should I stop and review the changes in my target market?' – annually is usually enough for most. And finally: 'How does your marketplace compare to overseas?' i.e.

'How advanced is your local market compared to elsewhere?' In some markets, technologically or in terms of market development, the UK is well ahead of most of the world, in others, it is not. For example, in the rest/care home market the UK or New Zealand could be ahead of America and Australia respectively, which means if you're based in the US or Australia it's probably worth hopping on a plane to visit a trade show or search a few overseas websites to see likely future trends in your market.

Suggested further reading

Another great tool to consider using when analysing potential new markets is the Porter's five forces model by Michael Porter. It goes beyond the normal competitive environment analysis and looks into factors such as the strength of buyers and suppliers alike.

O and T of SWOT analysis

As you likely know, SWOT stands for Strengths, Weaknesses, Opportunities and Threats. Strengths and Weaknesses are internal factors, so they are addressed in the next chapter, internal analysis. Opportunities and Threats are external factors, i.e. they are things over which you have no control. For example, it is not a strength of yours that people want to buy locally-made products, that is an opportunity.

Most of the external factors, both opportunities and threats, will often come down to six things, known as PESTEL: Political, Economic, Social, Technological, Environmental and Legal. Some things might come down to events and one-off opportunities, such as the Olympic Games, which was a one-off opportunity for some businesses and a one-off threat for others.

Brexit would be a common political factor in recent times, which is an opportunity for some and a threat for others, sometimes even both. Economic factors include exchange rates, global or local recessions, industry growth and interest rates. Social factors focus on people including an ageing population, the ethnicity mix of the market and general fashions and tastes. When we think about technological factors we're thinking of the Internet, advancements in high-speed broadband and WiFi access, 3D printing, even faster global air travel. Environmental factors often come down to two main areas: the 'green dollar' where some people and businesses choose to spend their money with environmentally aware businesses, and natural disasters. Legal is the final factor, covering topics such as health and safety legislation and anything around compliance.

As mentioned before, some factors offer your business both an opportunity and a threat at the same time. It is good to spend time quarterly or annually to redo a PESTEL analysis on your marketplace.

Competitor analysis

Thanks to the digital and online age, analysing your opposition is easier today than it's ever been in business before. The more you know about your main competitors the easier it is to defend your turf so to speak. In-depth competitor research can prove invaluable, but beware of analysis paralysis.

We've made it simple for you in this book to analyse a direct competitor. Using the Venn diagram, list in the top section all the advantages you have over them as a business. In the bottom section list all the advantages they have over your business – be honest. Then in the middle overlap section, list all the things you are both good at when compared to most of your shared competitors. Repeat this exercise for as many of your main direct competitors as you can, usually three to six competitors.

You now have two options to strengthen your proposition versus each of your analysed competitors. Either pick something from the bottom section and write down an action to help you match their strength in that area, thus moving that point from the bottom up to the middle section in the diagram in order to weaken their proposition when compared to you. Or pick a shared strength in the middle section and write down an action to implement to become better than them in that area – and so move that point from the middle to the top section, thus strengthening your proposition versus them.

Figure 3 Competitor analysis Venn diagram

Take action in your marketing plan

Target market:

- Define three clear target markets for your main business offering and ensure there is a big enough target market to ensure your business can succeed.

Market analysis:

- Especially for your main target markets, ask yourself the four questions from this chapter.
- Consider *Porter's Five Forces*.

O and T of SWOT analysis:

- List all the PESTEL factors that may create Opportunities.
- List all the PESTEL factors that may create Threats.
- Then list any actions required to leverage those opportunities or protect against those threats.

Competitor analysis:

- For at least your top three competitors, use the Venn diagram principles to compare them to your business.
- Then pick one item to 'move up' as explained above.

5. Marketing proposition: internal analysis

Getting your internal marketing proposition right is critical or you will waste your marketing communication efforts promoting the wrong proposition to the marketplace.

Key points in this chapter:

- Setting your marketing goals
- S and W of SWOT analysis
- Competitive advantage
- Market positioning
- Unique selling proposition
- Product, price, place, promotion
- Measuring what matters

Setting your marketing goals

If you're not aiming at a specific goal, your communication efforts will likely become worthless. You'll be back in Stephen Covey's Quadrant One doing a bunch of 'marketing stuff' that's not going to contribute much value to your business or customers.

There are countless ways to set goals for your marketing. We've found over the years that the simpler the goal, the easier it is to focus on and the easier it is to communicate to your whole team. Hence the easiest marketing goals you could set would be either sales/turnover goals, or gross profit goals.

Roughly a third of the businesses we observe around the world break those overall goals down into the number of units to sell of your core products or services, the number of projects you need to complete, or the number of active customers you need to have. By breaking your goal down into easy numbers, you make it easier to measure progress and easier to align your different divisions across the business to those same goals.

S and W of SWOT analysis

Opportunities and Threats were covered in the previous chapter under external analysis. Strengths and Weaknesses are internal factors, they are things over which you have direct control. Beware of the common mistake of confusing internal weaknesses with external threats. You can't directly influence external threats.

A starting point for strengths is to list down all the things over which you have control that you are good at. From a marketing perspective, strengths will be anything about your team, your branding, your product range, your price point, your market knowledge, your industry experience, the quality of your marketing planning, your measuring activity, your website, even your marketing budget, i.e. anything that makes you good.

Then repeat the exercise for all your weaknesses, listing down all the factors that stop you dominating the market fully, including your team, your experience, your location, your size, your team's skills, your knowledge of the market or competitors, the size of your database, your branding, your marketing skills, even your team's sales skills etc.

Competitive advantage

There's nothing mysterious or complicated about competitive advantage. It simply means 'what factors give you an advantage versus most of your competition?' In common parlance, these are your points of difference. A simple way to consider your competitive advantage is to revisit your strengths and note down any strengths that you have over most of your opposition. A great question to ask is: 'Why would customers choose you over other suppliers?' If you really are unsure, ask your sales team what your customers like about you.

Top tip

If you really get stuck with this, simply get out on the road (or phone) with your customers, ask them what they like about you and what they'd like to see improved. They'll probably be happy to share their ideas and opinions!

Market positioning

Put simply, market positioning simply means where you sit in the marketplace compared to others. If you were in the car industry, would you be a Rolls Royce near the top of the market or a Soviet-era Lada, near the bottom? The advantage being high on the echelon means you're likely to have higher profit margins, which means if there's an economic downturn, you've probably got cash in the bank to see you through. If you're at the budget end and the market collapses, you may not have much cash profit to ride out the storm. On the other side of the coin, if you're at the top end and there's a recession, people may skip your product to opt for mid-level solutions. There are pros and cons at each level and you need to be aware of them in your industry. Moving down is easy. Moving up is really hard.

An example

Porsche is one of the best-known examples. When they came out with a 'poor man's Porsche', as it became known, they realised that there was a huge market of potential customers who really wanted a Porsche but couldn't afford one. Unfortunately for them, this worked very well. As a result the market was flooded with cheaper Porsches and by putting these 'lesser' Porsches out on the road they forgot the real target market they served. Their ideal target market enjoyed the semi-exclusive nature of the brand. As such the 'real' Porsche customers left the entire Porsche range in their droves when it came to renewing their car the next time around. This is an example of brand contamination from a market positioning perspective.

Unique Selling Proposition (USP)

It has been globally taught for decades that in a marketplace the size of Britain, Europe or North America, you can't survive in business long term unless there is some unique reason why you exist: one thing you do that no one else can do. We have seen, however, that in smaller economies such as Australia and New Zealand there are plenty of companies surviving without being particularly unique. That said, one thing we're sure of is that regardless of your market size, having a clear USP invariably makes you more profitable by focusing your team on adding unique value to your customers and by reducing your customers' potential fixation on price. Thinking about your major opposition, is there one thing of value to customers that you can do that they can't do? Often you'll find it's a mixture of things. For example you might be the only UK-based, family-owned company that specialises in X, Y and A, and that delivers within

12 hours day or night. Your USP can be written in bullet point form, a long paragraph, an extra-long sentence. Please note: we're not talking about a tagline, slogan or strapline here, that is part of branding.

For example, if you decide that one of your USPs is speed, then your speed of proposal response, speed of delivery, speed of turnaround etc. is all part of that USP and so it's relevant to every division in your company. Consistency is king when it comes to developing a strong brand in people's minds.

Top tip

It is really worthwhile to test your assumptions about your USP with your own team and with your paying customers – after all it's what your customers are paying for. Then ensure your entire team, from director to part-time floor cleaner, know your main USP points.

The first P of marketing: Product

This comes from the original Marketing Mix or 4 Ps of Marketing several decades ago: product, price, place and promotion. Since the growth of service companies and different distribution models, the first P is sometimes an S for service and the third P is sometimes a D for distribution. Hence the 4 Ps is not used so much in marketing these days, as for some it has become 2 Ps, an S and a D! What's more there are over 30 Ps these days including people, (brand) personality, perseverance and presentation to name a few. People also refer to the 4 Cs of Marketing, with Customer replacing Product; Cost replacing Price; Convenience replacing Place; Communication replacing Promotion. When it comes to your marketing proposition, it's important to market the things you do best, the things you are passionate about and profitable with, the things that will best move your business forward. That doesn't mean you won't sell minor products or services as well, it simply means you should proactively focus on your key products or services first. Noting down your core three to five products or services before you plan your marketing campaigns is a useful thing to do – so you stay focused on your core business. To alter your focus on Product (or Service) and instead focus on Customer, means to become customer driven such as the customer-led flexibility of Subway sandwiches as opposed to the product-led inflexibility of the Ford Model T.

The second P of marketing: Price

Pricing is a huge subject that could fill a book by itself. Most people understand the principle of price versus demand: if the price of something rises, the demand often drops; if the price for something falls, the demand often rises. There are exceptions to these rules, called giffen goods, where a lower price can negatively impact demand (e.g. if apples were only 5 cents or 5 pence a kilo people may not trust them), and we see examples every year of people being reassured by higher prices (e.g. especially technology items such as smart phones). However, over 95 per cent of the time the main price-to-demand rule applies.

You are likely an expert in your industry or prospective industry and we expect you will have already looked at the pricing of comparative products to decide where you fit. Three things to remember:

- Always be deliberate with your pricing rather than leaving it to chance and therefore to others to decide for you.

- If you are going to discount or give something away, always tell the customer the true value of your generosity so they can share that goodwill story with others.
- If you intend to use the more modern Cost instead of Price, consider the full cost breakdown to customers including the time cost to switching to or from you, even opportunity costs.

> **Top tip**
>
> We've met literally hundreds of businesses over the years who have claimed the following: 'We decided to launch our product at a lower price, accepting the lower profit margins, in order to make up the lower profit through selling higher volumes.' The mistake made is the assumption that just lowering your prices will immediately make people discover your product or service: you also need to use effective communication tactics to let all those extra required people know your prices are lower than others.

Another pricing concept we'd love to highlight here is the economic principle, price elasticity: the correlation in your marketplace between price and demand.

For example, cigarettes, alcohol and petrol are price elastic, you can stretch the price without drastically impacting demand. At the other extreme are commodity products such as regular bleached, white table salt (not healthy pink Himalayan salt). Someone walking down a grocery aisle is likely to shift their loyalty on a product such as this, for a few pence or cents. What you need to consider for your industry, especially for your core products or services, is the likely impact on demand if there were a change in price.

The third P of marketing: Place

As mentioned, this is more commonly viewed as Distribution, or more recently Convenience. Place used to refer to your place of doing business such as a shop, but countless businesses choose instead to import goods or services and have resellers sell them across multiple 'places', in order to gain leverage. Whether you sell from one place or you distribute indirectly through multiple places, there is more flexibility these days. 'Convenience' refers to how easy or convenient you make it for end users and customers to access your product or service. In the digital age this is becoming an increasingly important area to consider, especially as people are less patient than before. This is well worth a discussion with your whole team about whether you should be making your products or services more convenient to access, including the challenging debate of ways to sell directly to customers while also supporting a reseller network.

The fourth P of marketing: Promotion

As we've already seen, the old style of marketing viewed running promotions as a tactic and while this can work in the short term, the better terminology these days is Communication. Such is its importance, the next two chapters focus on it.

Measuring what matters

This is one of the most critical areas of marketing today. Due to the faster pace of business, measuring in order to make smarter decisions is paramount. You can measure anything in marketing these days. Learn what to measure and how to measure it, to stay proactive in your marketing.

Anything you measure, when watched, will likely improve. Elton Mayo found this in 1927 when he did the Hawthorne experiments. He went to two production lines in the factory and said to one, 'Guys, we're just going to observe you over the next three months just to see how you operate.' To the other identical production line he said nothing. Because the first group knew they were being measured, there was a noticeable improvement in performance.

There are two things you can measure in your marketing. You can measure input or lead measures (read *The 4 Disciplines of Execution* by Sean Covey, Chris McChesney and Jim Huling) and there are result-based or lag measures. Most businesses are good at measuring lag measures because they've got accounting software or CRM (Customer Relationship Management) database software that does it semi-automatically. Measuring overall sales, overall profit margins, the average value per order, how many enquiries you get, are all good examples of lag measures.

Businesses that use worthwhile lag measures should continue to do so, but they must also look to increase the number of lead measures in order to become proactive and more astute in planning their marketing tactics. Anything to do with leads or conversion rates are lag measures. Anything to do with actions or inputs is a lead measure.

An example

British Airways. Their slogan was: 'The world's favourite airline'. Towards the end of the last century they started losing market share. They found that a cause was a reduction in repeat customers and a reduction in referrals (Pillars four and five). While the result was a drop in those two pillars, the cause (lead measure) was in part due to people missing flight connections, which in turn was influenced by them taking too long to service and prepare a plane for take off after it had landed somewhere. The senior team then had every country manager focus on that one lead measure or cause, i.e. they measured the action they had control over. They then worked hard to meet their pre-set standards on plane turnarounds, which minimised late take offs, which minimised missed connections, which minimised unhappy customers, which increased repeat customers and referrals, which led to a growth in market share globally.

British Airways were able to grow their market share simply by focusing on one key action-based lead measure. What action-based or lead measures should you use to impact your sales and results?

Take action in your marketing plan

Setting your marketing goals:

- Set your overall sales or gross profit goal for the year ahead.
- Break those down per month and/or into simpler goals.

S and W of SWOT analysis:

- Having listed your strengths, pick at least one key strength and write down an action point for what you can do to enhance it or protect it.
- Having listed your weaknesses, pick at least one and write down what you can do to minimise it.

Take action in your marketing plan, continued

Competitive advantage:

- List three to six key strengths you have versus most of your opposition.

Market positioning:

- Note if your core products or services sit at the top, middle or bottom of the market and think about the implications of that position.

Unique selling proposition:

- Work with your team and customers to determine your USPs then ensure you share them everywhere in all you do.

Product, price, place, promotion:

- Get clear on your core products/services, plan your pricing and consider price elasticity, consider place/distribution/convenience with your team and consider if promotions are appropriate.

Measure what matters:

- List down all the results-based (lag) measures you should be measuring: such as total sales, units sold of a specific product or service, gross profit margins, average sales value per purchase, website enquiries, enquiry to sales conversion rate and more.

- Then list down some lead (action-based) measures: things you have control over, that you know will impact the number of opportunities that you generate or your brand perception.

Nothing great was ever achieved without enthusiasm.

Ralph Waldo Emerson
philosopher and poet

6. Marketing communication: non-digital

While digital marketing and online marketing are the most spoken about topics in marketing these days, there is still a place for many of the more traditional marketing communication tactics. In fact in some industries non-digital tactics can appeal more to certain customers. The key is to know what is most relevant to your industry and if in doubt, ask your customers.

Key points of this chapter:

- Branding and printing
- Advertising
- Public relations
- Direct marketing
- Networking and alliances
- Direct selling and client management
- Training as a marketing investment
- Other marketing

Branding and printing

There are two sides of branding, just like there are two sides of marketing, proposition and communication. A way to view branding proposition is to think about the traditional way of branding cattle: where the brand on their hide stayed with them no matter what ranch or farm they went to. Another great way to think about the branding proposition is this: what is the long-term feeling or impression that a brand leaves in the hearts and minds of customers, long *after* the product or service has been consumed?

From a branding communication perspective, we mostly focus on the ways we can visually portray our brand(s). It goes without saying that this is one of the easiest areas to influence the way people perceive you: through your logo, your fonts, your colours, and your business cards.

This is one area of marketing communication which is a fairly level playing field between SMEs and larger businesses. A large corporation might spend a million pounds on redesigning a logo and brand, but it won't look a thousand times better than a smart SME who uses a good designer and pays a couple of thousand. Good quality print is good quality print, and the cost difference between good and great is minimal. When you think about the golden rules around branding and printing, consistency is king. You also get judged by your weakest link – your most poorly printed flyer, business card or image – so be tough on yourself with this. If you intend to have sales reps meeting customers face to face you will need to invest in branding and printing.

Advertising (non-digital)

Traditional advertising for SMEs usually consists of industry magazines, local publications, or advertising in another organisation's newsletters, etc. Advertising in a relevant industry publication can build your brand, in part due to the connection between whatever the publication is and your brand, plus it may or may not generate leads. While some SMEs pay for advertising because it saves you time, we do not recommend this becomes your reason for doing so: you will likely waste your hard-earned profits. On the flipside, advertising is often expensive, harder to measure and you pay for it regardless of whether people see it or respond to it.

While businesses like Coca-Cola and Procter & Gamble prove each year that traditional advertising still works, for SMEs it is often too broad a brush and untargeted to be a core marketing tactic. In addition, to make an impact with advertising it can become never ending in terms of spending levels. One thing that used to get us both up in the early days of our organisation, THE Marketing Company, was to stop business owners wasting their hard-earned profit on lazy advertising (unfocused, expensive advertising simply aimed at 'getting your name out there').

A more affordable area of advertising is signage. You see it on building sites, billboards, vehicles and showrooms alike. It's a very affordable way to show people where you have jobs on, where you travel to in their local area and where you're located. This is a far more common use of advertising for SMEs.

If you have a limited marketing budget overall, you must stay smart and focused with any advertising you use, as well as being prepared to measure the results fully. If you're not prepared to do this, then skip advertising and try another tactic.

Top tip

Too few businesses use internal signage in their workplace to motivate their own team. Consider better signage in your workplace to reinforce your USP, your brand and to share customer testimonials. A more motivated team will always serve your customers better, thus helping with Pillars four and five.

Public relations (PR)

Public relations is an ideal and underused marketing tactic for SMEs. While it drifts into the digital space these days in the form of content marketing, PR is just as relevant today as always. While people tend not to trust adverts as much today, PR can build long-term brand trust. Examples include public speaking, sending press releases to industry magazines and websites, sponsorship, charitable contribution, local community participation, even media commentary.

An example

If you've done something innovative for a client, why don't you get somebody to write an article about you helping the client create this massive productivity or safety improvement? You gain, the client gains and the industry learns from it. Better still most industries are calling out for relevant content, especially if it comes for free.

Public speaking is an ideal way to position yourself as an expert, especially as most people (possibly including your competitors) fear speaking in public. If you've got advice to share, speaking at the front of a room at an industry forum to people in your target market can work wonders. The fact that you stood up already suggests you're an expert. Speaking to a small group of specifiers like architects, while giving them free cakes, to share your story, can also be highly effective. If you're keen to try this tactic, there are organisations such as Toastmasters International (toastmasters.org) which offer affordable public speaking, confidence and leadership development training.

Sponsorship as a form of PR comes in many forms including commercial sponsorship of an event, of an event speaker or segment, or of a team or organisation. The new approach to sponsorship is focused on longer term partnerships i.e. pick something you're likely to support for three to five years minimum.

Charitable contribution has changed dramatically in recent times. The old-fashioned approach used to be that you kept your good causes secret, aiming not to gloat. Things have changed because many charities are fighting for attention and they too have limited marketing budgets and demanding stakeholders. So if you support a charity or cause, assuming you have written permission from them, why not shine a light on what that cause is? Share an article or share a photo with your team, to get people to think about whatever the charity does. Your primary goal should be to support any cause with an open heart and mind and any marketing gain is secondary to that, especially as people can thankfully see through disingenuous actions.

Top tip

Picking a suitable cause should ideally include your entire team. It can become an incredibly unifying and motivating exercise for your team, in turn helping them serve your customers better. When staff members come to work with

> a bigger reason 'why' (read Simon Sinek's *Start With Why*), they will probably become more productive and successful.

Local community participation, such as helping out when there has been a flood, is a good thing to do as a team, as a business and as a person. There is no harm in wearing your company clothing when doing so either, to build goodwill in the local market among your staff, your suppliers, your future employees and your local customers.

Not many SMEs are confident enough to do media commentary, which is to position yourself as the go to person for the media within a certain industry or geographic area. This usually involves you actively commenting on local and online news sites, calling local reporters with new ideas for stories, and being available for comment on any related business news item.

In summary, while advertising often seems like shouting, PR is more like whispering.

An example

After the 2011 Canterbury earthquakes, like others around New Zealand, a small group of us got together to do a fundraising concert on behalf of the region we were living in, Taranaki. We wanted to show the people of Canterbury that we cared. Fortunately we had a member of staff who had recently run a concert for the people of Samoa after a Tsunami so he had the contacts to access the bands we needed.

Having agreed to underwrite the concert to ensure the New Plymouth District Council gave us their premier concert venue for free, we were listed as one of many sponsors in some of the advertising. In no way did we expect a direct pay back, as with true PR, we simply wanted to do something positive.

> Somewhat surprisingly it did pay back years later, when the NZ Red Cross, recipients of the money we had raised, asked to do some customer service training with us.
>
> As stated, do something that feels right in PR and the direct payback is irrelevant.

Direct marketing

Direct marketing is highly targeted and therefore more suited to many SMEs than most traditional advertising, provided you are clear about your target market. It includes direct mail, telemarketing, email marketing (covered in the next chapter), even posting your latest catalogue to customers. Please remember that this tactic works for both new customers and existing customers. In this digital and email age, a handwritten thank you card to an existing customer can work wonders for customer loyalty.

Telemarketing calls may not be your favourite thing to receive, but it is one of the most common forms of direct marketing for SMEs, especially to existing customers. It can help with market research, educating your customers and for lead generation. Telemarketing is also a good tactic to use after you've generated hot leads from a trade show.

Networking and alliances

Networking face-to-face (we'll cover social media networking in the next chapter) is what your salespeople may do at industry and local business events. This involves showing up at an event rather than sponsoring or exhibiting at it. Networking can build great long-term contacts, especially within a smaller community or industry. For a small investment of time or money, it can be very beneficial, especially to learn more about the local marketplace. As we've delivered countless keynote speeches at conferences on this subject: please remember that networking is equally focused on existing contacts as it is about finding new contacts. To network confidently is a skill that can be learned by even the shyest of people.

Strategic alliances are one step further. Ask yourself: 'Are there any individuals or organisations you can buddy up with to leverage off each other's brand, contacts or knowledge?' Could you share the cost of exhibiting at an expo? If you wanted to do a direct mail campaign to existing contacts and the biggest cost was the cost of postage, if two businesses put flyers into the same envelope, you'd halve distribution costs and leverage from one another's brands. The golden rules around this are making sure you have alignment in terms of brand values. The risk to either party from any alliance is if there is a brand clash. There needs to be a strong level of trust from both parties.

An example

As a supplier of safety gear you could form a short-term alliance with a construction design expert and run a series of road shows together. They stand and speak about new design innovation, while you speak about new safety regulations or PPE (Personal Protection Equipment). Both of you promote the event to new and existing customers, sharing the cost and effort.

Direct selling and client management

Despite the traditional order of the words in the phrase 'sales and marketing', sales, technically, is a subset of marketing. It is the human-to-human side of marketing. If you are in a complex industry, if you sell something very conceptual or even major capital equipment, and there needs to be some element of customer education or detailed explanation, then direct selling is an ideal marketing tactic. A common area to review for SMEs right now is the structure of their sales teams as well as the natural behavioural tendencies of their sales teams, using tools like Extended DISC®, to ensure each team member is in their most suitable sales functions.

Proactive ongoing client, or account, management is key to a long-term customer retention. We need to be clear here: there is a difference between customer service and client management. Customer service is how you treat your customers while you're in the process of selling to them or while you're delivering your product or service to them. As such it is a reactive action, not proactive, and while important, it is rarely a long-term differentiator in a business. Your customers expect good customer service as part of what they pay for, the only time they really talk about it is if it's terrible!

What can really make a difference to loyalty and brand perception is when you actively lead the relationship with existing customers. Giving people gifts at the end of the year to say thank you for your support is an example of client management. Sending a newsletter once a quarter to people saying 'here's some relevant information for you' is another example, as is having salespeople follow a call cycle that adds value to resellers. This is where sales and marketing definitely tie together. Please ensure that your marketers in your business are aligned to the sales team on call cycles, gifting, product launches and promotions.

As a general rule of client or account management, most businesses have A (Gold), B (Silver) and C (Bronze) tier customers, while others break it down further than that. The A/Gold customers get better gifts, more active support and more visits than your C/Bronze customers who receive more email communication.

An example

This is one of our favourite demonstrations of proactive client management. A used car salesman from the American Midwest in the 1980s used just one form of client management when someone bought a vehicle, while his colleagues had no client management. He noted down their birthday and sent them a handwritten birthday card every year. Back then people changed cars on average every seven years, so it cost him about seven dollars over that time period. The result was that so many customers came back to him (Pillar four) and referred others to him (Pillar five) that it ended up taking him three days per month simply to write birthday cards, while consistently outselling everyone else!

There's a thousand case studies like that from around the world. Proactive effort goes a long way, no matter how simple or expensive it is. A golden rule to keep in mind is the 90 Day Rule. This states that after 90 days if you haven't proactively contacted a customer, they may forget that you care or they will likely forget what makes you special and so are unlikely to refer to you. Proactive contact is initiated by you, rather than simply responding to client enquiries or orders.

Customer surveys are also forms of client management. Asking someone for their opinion not only shows respect but it can make them feel more connected to your brand. The best question to ask in a survey these days is the Net Promoter Score Question which can be worded: 'On a scale of 1 to 10 with 1 being never and 10 being all the time, how likely would you be to refer us to others?' Why this question is so valuable is because it measures intended behaviour rather than simply an opinion. You see, by asking if they would refer you you're actually asking them if they are happy to be associated with you. Customers who score you 9 or 10 out of 10 are called net promoters (they are likely to refer you), 7s and 8s are neutral (they'll say nothing), and anyone from 1–6 is called a detractor (either they're actively saying bad things about you or when asked they're more likely to share a bad comment).

Training as a marketing investment

In *The One Minute Manager* by Ken Blanchard and Spencer Johnson, the authors found after decades of research with countless organisations – small, medium and large – that companies spend more time and money on maintaining their buildings and their equipment than they do on maintaining and developing their people.

It's absurd, because when you ask most managers and business owners: 'What's your number one asset?', 'Our people' is the most common response. An important fact to note is that many of the most successful companies in their industry, such as Coca-Cola, Proctor & Gamble and McDonald's, invariably put more into developing their people than all others in their industry. This could just be a lucky coincidence. We think not.

Most SMEs don't have set training budgets that impact their marketing success such as sales, marketing and customer service skills, so we recommend using some of your marketing budget instead. As common sense would tell you, superior sales skills will invariably lead to high sales conversion (Pillar one) and higher profit margins (Pillar three).

Other marketing

In this section we will whip through other semi-common non-digital marketing tactics. There are countless other tactics, too numerous to fit into this *Authority Guide*. Our view is that if you think it will help at least one of the pillars, think about it. If you're unsure, dismiss it as a distraction.

- Events, expos and trade shows can be expensive (in both time and money) but, well planned, they can help you reach high numbers of target customers. Be sure to research and possibly even visit future events in advance. Please remember that if it's a three-day event, it likely means it's probably going to cost you three days of planning and three days of follow-up. So a three-day event means it's really a nine-day event.
- Make sure your premises motivate your staff members and customers alike. People should feel good coming to work and this will reflect in the way they interact with customers. Once a year it's worth looking to freshen up your workplace, especially if you involve your team in the planning.
- Running promotions is a good way to generate short-term sales growth but please ensure two things: that you're fully aware of the impact any discount or promotion has on your profit margins (Pillar three) and that you don't create a habit within your customers so they only buy from you when a promotion is running.

Top tip

Verify that every member of your team knows how to correctly respond to the question: 'So where do you work?', i.e. that everyone has a 30-second spiel or elevator pitch. A secret worth mentioning here is that the best 30-second spiels are only 12–15 seconds long! They simply need to include your first name, your company, your role and one thing you like about your role or one thing the company does differently to others. If appropriate, add in one thing about you personally such as about your family or favourite pastime.

- Corporate clothing is affordable and ideal if you want to stand out at an event as a team, plus it suggests brand consistency to potential customers.
- Guerrilla or stealth marketing can be fun and effective. If traditional advertising is like a war of attrition guerrilla marketing is like guerrilla warfare, hence the name. It generally involves a small team of people who, for a short burst of time, try to have the biggest impact they can. It can be a great way to launch a product or service into a small geographic market. It can also be a really motivating team activity, as we experienced first hand when promoting a joint business conference back in 2006.

An example

A pizza restaurant could hire a group of students to take free slices of pizza, together with a discount voucher, up and down the street on a Friday evening and in a very short space of time countless people would not only taste their pizza, but they would have an incentive to come and buy some.

- Viral marketing in the physical world is something that requires thought and planning. Sometimes it works and sometimes not. We once helped a new café owner, in the pre-social media days, try to switch the public's perception of them from seeing them as an ice cream shop into being seen as a great café. With next to nothing to invest into marketing we suggested they ask their coffee supplier for some free coffee beans, and that they texted 20 of their most connected friends with this message: 'Free coffee at ABC café, Wednesday after 3pm, pass it on!' It didn't take long for people to hear about it – there was a queue around the block, the local newspaper came to see them and do a front page spread on their re-launch and in one afternoon countless people knew that they sold great coffee.

- Loyalty reward programmes can assist with repeat customers (Pillar four), provided the rewards are of value, the programme is easy to run or outsourced, and it is legal and appropriate for customers to receive rewards.

> ### Take action in your marketing plan
>
> Branding and printing: list any items you may need to improve: logo, brand, slogan, business cards, brochures, flyers, letterheads, envelopes, photos, images and more.
>
> Advertising: consider any traditional advertising or signage options.
>
> Public relations: consider all the PR options that suit your business.
>
> Direct marketing: consider what options will work for you.
>
> Networking: pick one to three events your team should network at.
>
> Alliances: pick two to three organisations to sit down with and say 'I think there's a common way we could jointly add value to the market.'
>
> Direct selling: review the size and structure of your sales team.
>
> Client management: ensure you rank your existing customers correctly and proactively manage them accordingly.
>
> Training: consider what sales, customer service and marketing skills your team need to maximise your marketing success.
>
> Other marketing: check through the section above and pick any actions.

7. Marketing communication: digital

Digital marketing is the growth area of marketing communication. Online marketing is a subset of digital marketing and simply focuses on factors where you need to be connected online. This area moves very fast these days and you should keep reading in this area to truly stay up to date.

Key points of this chapter:

- Websites and online
- SEO and SEM
- Social media and content marketing
- Mobile marketing
- Marketing automation

Websites and online

The first comment we'd like to make on this topic is to stay flexible. Whether that's flexible with the software that is used to build your website (i.e. try to work with a web designer who uses an 'open' software such as WordPress), or flexible with which web development company you choose (i.e. you want to be able to switch from a supplier the moment they become outdated and inflexible), flexibility is king right now.

How things have quickly changed online:

- The first phase of website development was totally wrong, it was 'build it and they will come'. It was like building a shop in the middle of a desert and assuming someone's going to stumble across it.
- The next phase became the search engine optimisation (SEO) obsession: you've got to make sure people visit. This gave rise to lazy tactics like link farms and spamming on your website (such as having secret pages stacked full of keywords that visitors could not see but Google could) trying to trick Google. Websites were visited but often by the wrong people, while the right people tended to have poor website experiences.
- Phase three became: 'It's all about the visitor pathway, persuasive content and converting visitors.'
- These days it's about all three of those things, plus the integration with social media, content marketing, online advertising, as well as your long-term customer follow-up plan. One thing we're sure of in marketing is that the hype around 'the next big thing' is just around the corner.

Online technology is moving so fast these days that your next decision will ideally position you where you can move quickly elsewhere if there's something better. Gone are the days where you only looked to change your homepage every three years. These days it's common to see businesses overhaul the functionality and their homepage in a single month. In the past, when SMEs approached their web designers for a new landing page or change, the standard response was, 'That's fine, we'll schedule you in 10–14 days' time.' These days you can find an online landing page builder available and ready to roll within a matter of hours!

Below is a quick checklist for your website:

1. When someone lands on your website in just three seconds they need to know three things: who you are, why you're trustworthy and what exactly you do. Most websites we see around the world achieve two of these three things, but rarely all three in three seconds.

2. People are more impatient these days than ever before. As such they won't linger long to find out how great you are, much in the same way that when someone walks into a shop in a shopping centre, if the store doesn't have exactly what they want, they turnaround and walk out in a matter of seconds. Make sure it's easy for people to view your range or past projects for example.

3. The next thing to set is your primary macro conversion goal for your website, i.e. the number one thing you want a visitor to do once they visit (this will often be an online purchase or an online enquiry).

4. You then need to set your backup macro conversion goal, i.e. what you want them to do if they don't do your primary goal (such as to have them call you).

5. Then set a micro conversion goal, and backup micro conversion goal, for each and every page on your website. It sounds like a lot of work but if you're going to compete online, compete to win.

6. Make it logical where website visitors should go, don't make them scroll unnecessarily, and hold their hand through their visit so to speak.

7. What is your USP? Any visitor wants to be able to see that clearly stated AND demonstrated on your website. For example, if you claim to be the most technically skilled team

in the industry, we should see images of your team, a list of qualifications and customer testimonials stating that your team is highly skilled.

This brings us to an important online tip that applies across your website, social media and mobile marketing: customer testimonials. These are increasingly valued these days. You can barely leave an aircraft, a café or supermarket without being asked to give feedback. It's a part of life these days so your prospective customers expect to see feedback on your business. Please keep in mind the following hierarchy of trust with testimonials:

1. Video testimonials are the most trusted, due to their candid and 'real' nature.

2. Written testimonials with client photos or logos beside them are the second most trusted. The words they say are rarely as impactful as the person that said them.

3. Written testimonials with the person and company name are the third most trusted.

4. Testimonials without a name are the fourth level and are no longer trusted.

Please remember legally, and as a sign of respect, always get customer permission to use their words, logo or name. A common question we get is: 'If I list customer testimonials on my website, surely my competitors will steal them from me?' Our response to that is that typically: 'It's your best customers that you list online, so were you to lose them it'll likely be for a multitude of reasons and not simply because you listed them online. So be brave and look after every customer so well that they'll never leave you.'

Keep in mind when asking a client for written testimonials to ask if they'd like you to email them some suggested words to save them time – 80 per cent of the time they'll simply email back stating you can use your words exactly: that way your testimonials are better written, you get them approved quicker and you have a digital record of approval from the customer.

Top tip

A better way to think these days is that your website *isn't* yours. You own it, you pay for it, but it really belongs to your customers. The moment you make that mental switch, you'll realise everything you do should be aligned to better serving them. They're the ones that fund your business and indirectly fund your website. Keep your customers at the heart of all your online planning and you'll likely make far smarter decisions.

SEO and SEM

SEO and SEM (search engine marketing) is about getting people to find your website online. One key point with SEO is to remember that Google ranks each page on your website, not merely your website as a whole or homepage alone. Having visitors land on uncluttered landing pages is a proven and popular way to increase ongoing contact.

Google uses over 200 different algorithms (programs) to track over 1,900 different factors as to whether a webpage comes up first on the organic search on Google. You simply can't cheat Google – and if someone claims they know how to, they're probably lying (or else Yahoo and Bing would have likely caught up by now).

SEM combines SEO and paid online tactics. In terms of online advertising, what we like about Google AdWords is that unlike display advertising online or traditional newspaper advertising, you only pay when someone actually does something: you Pay Per Click. In the past 12 months Google has removed the AdWords column from the right-hand side and added a fourth paid ad at the top. If you wish to understand how the adverts are ordered, simply Google 'Google advert auction' and there are some great videos by Google about their Ad Rank process.

Online display advertising works like traditional advertising where you pay per impression and where the location of the advert must be very targeted.

Remarketing is growing in popularity with SMEs. That is where after someone visits a specific web page of yours, they are served up adverts from you elsewhere on the internet, such as on a news or weather website, as a reminder. What is great is that you can specifically target people based on what they did on your site. For example, if someone bought a piece of equipment online from you, you could remarket to them to buy a service contract. It is typically more expensive than AdWords but it is highly targeted and measurable.

Now we come to an area of online marketing that many SMEs get confused about in Direct Email Marketing: e-blasts/e-shots versus e-newsletters. E-newsletters are all about sharing news, tips and adding value, their purpose is to build customer loyalty (and so help Pillars four and five). E-blasts or e-shots are simply a form of targeted advertising where you tend to shout a single message or offer at the customer. Both add value to your marketing but be sure to use a combination of both, so you maintain customer loyalty. Relevancy is king in the online world: relevant tips, relevant advice and relevant offers at a relevant time.

Social media and content marketing

Your first consideration with social media has to be about the time-wasting potential for each of these channels, be it your time, an employee's time or an outsourced party's time. This should force you to ask the two critical questions. Firstly, which social media channels do your customers use regularly? Secondly, and just as importantly, when and how do they use those channels? (You don't want to spam people with your business brand through a channel they use to switch off from work.)

What's great about social media is that it is very trackable as a tool, and it's easy to test and measure what works on an ongoing basis to refine your approach. That said, it can take SMEs a lot longer to get significant pay back from their social media efforts so many should see this as a long-term tactic rather than a short-term one. Facebook, LinkedIn and Twitter are the big three channels for most countries, especially if businesses sell B2B.

Your main options are that you can post an article, video, or photo, you can comment on or like someone else's articles, photos or videos, and you can advertise through most social media channels. To help make you more time efficient with posting it is helpful to use tools such as Hootsuite where you can preload your posts so they drip feed out at pre-set times. Please keep in mind though that social media is 'social' in nature so people expect you to monitor your channels and respond in a timely fashion when they ask a question or make a comment.

A golden rule to follow if you outsource your social media activities is to ensure that you set clear goals for your social media partner to be measured against. The most important thing to measure in social media is engagement, i.e. how many people comment on your posts, like your posts or share your posts. 'Views' and 'followers' are less of a focus these days, especially as you can buy worthless followers easily.

LinkedIn is great for the B2B side of business. Its origin was people going for jobs and wanting to avoid tough gatekeepers and HR Managers. Suddenly you were able to contact people directly and through mutual warm contacts. In the beginning, people used to ask your contacts for introductions but few people can be bothered nowadays because they're so impatient. Once you have over 500 connections on LinkedIn it is hard for people to turn down a request to connect with you anyway. Hence the more active you are on social media, the easier it becomes.

Top LinkedIn tips

1. Complete your profile *fully*.

2. Connect with your clients.

3. Connect with industry influencers.

4. Join one to two groups and join in with their discussions.

5. Accept invitations from credible people and turn down random people.

6. Make comments on people's updates.

7. Follow great practitioners to learn and copy.

8. Keep your comments warm but professional.

9. When inviting someone to connect, ideally explain why you want to connect such as 'I've just read your book and I'd love to connect'.

Facebook's origin was C2C (consumer to consumer). Hence the first businesses to adopt Facebook as a core social media channel were often B2C businesses (business to consumer). Nowadays it's common for B2B companies to use Facebook daily also. The best way to think about it from a business perspective is to think: how can I entertain, educate or add value to the people who may refer to my business or may use our business in the future? The content should be friendly and relaxed and you must stay on top of your Facebook page to ensure you respond in a very timely fashion to comments made (ideally within an hour or two).

Top tip

The golden rule for businesses using Facebook when it comes to their posts is the 70/20/10 Rule. For every 100 posts you make, 70 of them should add value (education, helpful hints, free advice, not self-promotion), 20 should be you commenting and sharing other people's ideas. Then you earn the right to self-promote with the remaining 10.

At its origin Twitter was just basically a 140-character text message interacting between people. Celebrities, sports stars and political figures then found it was a quick way to communicate with their followers hourly. It has now evolved, with images and videos, to being a great way to communicate not only with your direct contacts but in a way that those connections may comment and retweet your news to all their connections. This point is at the heart of all social media: they all give you the opportunity to share something worthwhile with your contacts in a way that is easy for them to on-share, and in turn those people can on-share again. This is how your 'reach' through social media can grow exponentially.

YouTube is a great site to upload videos, as is Wistia or Vimeo. If you have great content to share such as instructional videos, product demonstrations, customer testimonials, hosting them somewhere is a must. As you build a loyal customer following, they will want to subscribe to your YouTube channel if you set one up.

> **Top tip**
>
> Rather than sending a customer to YouTube to watch a video, simply embed that video into your website or newsletter so when they finish watching it's your website or newsletter that they're staring at.

Pinterest and Instagram are both image-based channels, ideal for visual companies. Pinterest is like a pin board, where people follow a theme or subject of interest. For example, you say you're interested in baking cakes and you see people posting images relating to the subject matter you've chosen. Instagram, now owned by Facebook, is where you follow a brand, a company or a person to see their updates. Instagram has rapidly moved from a static image social media platform to being very video-based.

You can also advertise on most social media channels. What's great about them is that you can choose what type of person you want to have your adverts presented to (whereas Google AdWords are more defined by location and the search term only). Typically you can pay for this extra privilege, plus some forms of social media advertising are Pay Per Impression (PPI) rather than PPC.

Overall, the main investment into social media by SMEs is the investment of time: time to create the content, time to post the content, time to monitor and respond to comments and time to measure engagement.

Content marketing is about sharing helpful and engaging content across multiple channels including all forms of social media, industry forums, blogs, your website, even your newsletter. Please note that it is more common to host your blog on your own website, especially as it will help with SEO.

Content marketing example

Marcus Sheridan was the owner of River Pools in the US, selling fibreglass pools.

When the housing crisis hit in 2008, pool sales slowed massively.

With a limited marketing budget Marcus started posting useful tips on forum pages and social media, as well as commenting on other related websites and forums where people posted pool-related questions (everything from the chemicals use, to pool safety, to pool fencing, even pool maintenance).

Without pushing his company, Marcus grew a loyal following online through adding value to people.

Once the recession softened Marcus's business grew rapidly from the loyalty he'd built for free!

Marcus now even does keynote speaking around the world on content marketing strategies, such was his success!

Mobile marketing

Mobile marketing is one of the main growth areas within digital marketing due to the fact that people are rarely more than a few centimetres from a smart device these days and most people are comfortable combining their digital and physical lives. There are several areas of mobile marketing that are appropriate for

SMEs to consider. Remember that the key is to keep your customers at the centre of your thoughts when planning.

QR codes may not be cutting edge technology but people are comfortable with them and they do work to shift a customer from the physical world to the online world. They're ideal to take someone to a product reorder page on your website or a product demonstration or maintenance video from a flyer or brochure.

Text marketing may not be new either, but it's a great way to communicate in the retail or hospitality sectors or where you have very open relationships with your clients. Remember the golden online rule of 'relevancy': keep the content or offer relevant and people won't resent the intrusive nature of this medium.

Mobile apps are becoming more mainstream these days and as such more SMEs are creating them for their ongoing customers. Better still, gone are the days when it cost a six-figure sum to design an app. If you find an app creator (such as 3 Sided Cube in the UK) with existing software already built it may only cost you a monthly fee. A great example of a smaller business using an app is Allpress Coffee from New Zealand: the app helps you to find nearby cafés who use their coffee in the UK and around the world for that familiar caffeine fix!

Augmented reality (not just for Pokemon Go!) is also dropping in cost. The latest Ikea catalogue allows you to see a 3D digital image of a piece of furniture on your mobile device so you can 'see' it in your home before purchasing. As this technology becomes mainstream, the costs will fall, so as we say in our online mobile marketing courses, start thinking in this way today so you're ready when you need to take action in the future.

Marketing automation

This has been with us for many years, often in the form of auto responder email streams. The giant leaps now being taken in this area may lead to marketing automation becoming the standard for businesses of all sizes within a few short years. By combining visitor behaviour, target customer profiling and artificial intelligence, the opportunity for fully-scaled, fully-personalised automated marketing is available right here right now. Companies such as Salesforce are achieving huge strides for their customers around the world.

Finally, we can't leave mobile marketing without mentioning video content again. Google suggests that we're going to go from 40 per cent of mobile content consumed being videos to over 60 per cent, in a few short years. As we've stated before, speed is key, so go and create useful video content today: installation videos, helpful guides, meet the team videos, client testimonials. Better still, gone are the days of you needing a whole camera crew. While your corporate video should be professionally created, for short videos people often value 'real' over 'polished'.

> **Take action in your marketing plan**
>
> Websites and online: go through the website checklist (as shown on page 53), decide if you need a website overhaul, and use more testimonials.
>
> SEO and SEM: plan what SEO and SEM help you need (paid or unpaid) including remarketing, AdWords and Direct Email Marketing.
>
> Social media and content marketing: work with your team and customers to pick the right social media channels for your business and how often to post, apply the LinkedIn tips and Facebook posting rule and consider more content marketing options.
>
> Mobile marketing: ensure your website is mobile friendly and go through the list of mobile options above.
>
> Marketing automation: consider what automation would help you grow.

8. Implementing your plan

Time to look at ways to help you implement your business plan. Our core focus in all our training, be it our Marketing Boot Camp or our Sales Mastery Programme, is: 'What you do after the training in terms of action matters more than what you do during the training.' It is only through taking action that you will grow a business. A simple way to help with implementation is to make your overall, or broken-down goals, as visual as possible and speak about them as much as you can with your whole team. This keeps everyone focused on the right goals as well as motivating them to support your marketing efforts.

The first step to help with implementation is to pre-set your budget, to invest in it all. The general rule of thumb for setting a marketing budget is 3 per cent of expected turnover of the year ahead. At THE Marketing Company we find a more realistic starting point is 10 per cent of expected gross profit as this takes into account your margins and it reminds you that the purpose of marketing is to drive profit not just sales. Compare this starting point with what you invested last year into your marketing together with your goals and ambitions for the year ahead.

What does your marketing budget cover? The loose percentages above are based on it covering all costs in marketing, including outsourced services, but excluding wages and staff training. That said we always encourage that if people chose to invest in say, sales training, as part of their marketing, they should still try to keep the overall budget within the 3 per cent or 10 per cent guidelines.

Please also keep in mind that as your budget is set on future sales, you must monitor your sales and profits each month in case you need to amend your budget up or down.

Once you have set the overall budget, it is best to split that budget into each key area of marketing, based on the *importance* of that area, rather than the past spend in that area (using the same Stephen Covey thinking about 'importance' being the key factor).

Use the template at the end of this book or better still the free online template at THEmarketingcompany.com to set and split your marketing budget.

Now you have a budgeted marketing plan, you need to set deadlines. Many of us, when given a project from a school teacher, left it until the last minute to get things done, no matter how stressful that was. While this isn't the best long-term strategy, it does prove that most of us are good with deadlines! Hence, you now need to put timelines against your planned actions, so that you can make each of those actions SMART (Specific, Measurable, Achievable, Realistic and *Time-lined*). This is critical in order to hold yourself to account with the actions to implement.

Next you need someone to hold you to account. As we covered very early in this book, one of the ongoing challenges with SMEs when it comes to their marketing is that people often get distracted by the whirlwind of other duties so their marketing activities become sporadic. Peer pressure works, as does using a coach, mentor or fellow business owner or manager. Have them hold you to account on the actions you plan to complete, ideally offsite, each month to help you shift your mindset to working 'on' the business.

The next step to help you implement is to accept that change is inevitable: don't beat yourself up each month if you don't complete all your planned activities. The key is to complete the activities that add the most value to your business and to your customers, and push back the lower valued actions to a later month.

Finally, please remember that motivation and momentum are at the heart of everything in business, so celebrate your wins, no matter how small, and reward yourself and your team for achieving planned activities and campaigns even if the full results will only arrive in the future. This will keep your morale high and the momentum building.

> **Take action in your marketing plan**
>
> - Set your overall marketing budget.
> - Split your budget into each area of marketing using the online template.
> - Break down your actions into months of the year, ensuring any actions that are quarterly are written in four times.
> - Contact the person who will hold you to account.

> Behold the turtle. He makes progress only when he sticks his neck out.
>
> James B. Conant
> President of Harvard

Conclusion

Marketing is at the heart of business whether you plan proactively for it to work well, or whether you allow your business and team to remain reactive. The two critical sides to marketing are Marketing Proposition and Marketing Communication, with the proposition side being broken into external and internal factors, and the communication side being broken into non-digital and digital tactics.

Marketing should directly assist with driving business profit and success by ideally helping with all five of THE Marketing Company's Profit Pillars of Marketing™.

The first action for you to take is to download the marketing plan template from THEmarketingcompany.com (search: Authority Guide), or copy the simple template overview from this book, and then complete your plan for the year ahead.

We are always excited by every success story we hear about. We have received literally hundreds of amazing stories from past customers about how, by being more proactive in their marketing, they have led their businesses to amazing success. What is always more important to us however, is the impact those successful businesses have had on their owners, their teams and their communities. We've heard countless stories of people achieving fairer SME shareholder returns, being able to send their children to higher education and the life-changing impact it has had on them, the ability to hire more staff in a shaky local economy meaning their employees have kept their homes, as well as the charities and good causes they have been able to help with their extra profits. In fact some of the charities we have helped with their marketing have literally saved lives and families as a result of taking action in their marketing and we feel privileged to have played a small part in that process.

The technologies will change, different channels of marketing communication (such as different social media options) will come and go, but what will stay the same are the five Profit Pillars of Marketing™ and the universal business law of serving others. That is why all businesses exist. At the heart of marketing is the customer. If we serve them well, we succeed. We cannot succeed however without serving them well on every interaction, through all of our marketing, through all of our sales interactions, through every email, through every visit. We are literally only as good as our last contact with each customer.

We once again congratulate you on choosing to read this *Authority Guide*. May this book be the start or continuation of your marketing learning. Keep learning, whether it's through articles, books, forums – even our online webinars. Do share your successes with us so we can continue to inspire others to grow and make a difference in the world.

Remember that the future of marketing and business success will likely come from economies of speed: speed to learn, speed to apply, speed to measure and speed to improve. Action is everything: so take action right now before the pages have even closed fully!

The TMC Authority Guide Marketing Plan Template™

Marketing goals	Overall	By month	Broken down
Target market	1	2	3
Market analysis	1	2	3
Opportunities	P E S T E L	Threats	P E S T E L
Competitor analysis	1	2	3
	We do better	We do better	We do better
	We do better	We do better	We do better
	They do best	They do best	They do best
Strengths		Weaknesses	
Competitive advantage		Marketing positioning	

Unique selling position			
Price, service, customer		Price, cost	
Place, distribution, convenience		Promotion, communication	
Branding and printing			
Advertising			
Public relations			
Direct marketing			
Networking and alliances			
Direct selling and client management			
Training			
Other marketing			
Website and online			
SEO and SEM			
Social media and content marketing			
Mobile marketing			
Marketing automation			

Budget	Marketing budget overall
Split into:	
Branding and printing	
Advertising	
Public relations	
Direct marketing	
Networking and alliances	
Direct selling and client management	
Training	
Other marketing	
Websites and online	
Social media and content marketing	
Mobile marketing	
Marketing automation	
Total	

> Theory is splendid but until put into practice, it is valueless.
>
> **James Cash Penney**
> **founder of J. C. Penney**

About the authors

Members of the New Zealand Marketing Association, affiliated to the Chartered Institute of Marketing, Jo and Ambrose Blowfield started THE Marketing Company in 2004. They have since taken the company international, training over 6,000 businesses across Australasia, the UK, Europe and North America, while pioneering numerous unique training programmes along the way from their marketing boot camp, to 12-week and 12-month sales programmes, to their global interactive LiveOnline training. Driven by a passion to help SMEs to achieve greater returns through improving their marketing planning and through mastering sales conversations, their philosophy is to teach others to fish for themselves rather than do the fishing for clients.

Jo Blowfield developed her street smarts in marketing, sales and customer service from the music industry, to travel, to accounting, invariably rising to leadership roles quickly. Her passion for helping others knows no bounds and her energy is as contagious as it is inspiring. She's even juggled this with two high achieving daughters. LinkedIn: linkedin.com/in/jo-blowfield-a6274313/

Ambrose Blowfield completed a bilingual honours degree in International Business with French from Aston University in the UK (rated one of the best bilingual business degrees in Europe) and a Certificate in Business Administration from Grenoble Graduate Business School in France. He was then one of the chosen few from thousands to join global marketing giant Proctor & Gamble in the UK. In Sydney he started at Australia's then leading recruitment firm Morgan & Banks, followed by the world's leading financial and accounting recruitment specialist Robert Half International. He then worked at two leading New Zealand companies before joining Jo in THE Marketing Company. LinkedIn: https://www.linkedin.com/in/ambrose-blowfield-6401549/

Who is THE Marketing Company?

THE Marketing Company has trained over 6,000 SMEs around the world from the UK, across Europe, to North America, Australia and New Zealand.

They offer one of the widest ranges of sales and marketing training solutions in the world, across multiple delivery methods: face-to-face, LiveOnline™ (highly interactive live learning), PureOnline™ (self-led flexible learning) and blended learning. All of it is geared to help you grow your business consistently. Below are their main unique solutions:

1. The Essential Marketing Boot Camp™ – you walk away with a prioritised, time-lined, challenged marketing plan in just one day.

2. The Persuasive Selling Process™ – advanced, world-class, sales course helping you to master conversations, overcome objections and sell more profitably.

3. The Intensive Sales Accelerator Programme™ – 12 B2B sales topics in 12 weeks to build your confidence and broad sales skills.

④ The Sales Mastery Programme™ – 12-month advanced programme to master your mindset and skills for every client interaction.

Free high-value webinars and sales and marketing tips newsletter available on THEmarketingcompany.com

Free tips through LinkedIn and Facebook (search THE Marketing Company).

Bibliography

Blanchard, K. and Johnson, S. (2011) *The One Minute Manager: Increase productivity, profits and your own prosperity*. HarperCollins.

Covey, S. (2004) *The 7 Habits of Highly Effective People.* Simon and Schuster.

Covey, S., McChesney, C. and Huling, J. (2016) *The 4 Disciplines of Execution: Achieving your wildly important goals.* Free Press.

Gerber, M. (2001) *The E-myth Revisited: Why most small businesses don't work and what to do about it.* HarperBusiness.

Porter, M. (1998) *The Competitive Strategy: Techniques for analysing industries and competitors.* Free Press.

Ries, A. and Trout, J. (1994) *The 22 Immutable Laws of Marketing.* Profile Books.

Sinek, S. (2011) *Start With Why: How great leaders inspire everyone to take action.* Portfolio.

Waitley, D. (1992) *The Psychology of Winning.* Warner Books.

You miss 100 per cent of the shots you don't take.

Wayne Gretzky
ice hockey legend

Other Authority Guides

The Authority Guide to Publishing Your Business Book: Take your business to a new level by becoming an authority in your field

Sue Richardson

Looking for a way to grow your business?

Publishing expert, Sue Richardson, shows you how to use your expertise, knowledge and experience to become a published authority in your field and gain the visibility you and your business needs. This *Authority Guide* will help you to create a plan that ensures you write and publish the right book for your business.

The Authority Guide to PR for Small Businesses:
Use the power of public relations and the media to reach your target customer and grow your business

Steve Bustin

Get media coverage and grow your business through PR with this practical guide.

Any business wanting to reach new customers should be embracing public relations to spread their key messages. If you don't, your competitors will. This *Authority Guide* shows you how to grab the headlines (for all the right reasons), reach huge audiences and grow your business by accessing the media to tell your story.

The Authority Guide to Marketing Your Business Book: 52 easy-to-follow tips from a book PR expert

Chantal Cooke

Want to get your business book flying off the shelves?

It's never too soon to start thinking about how to market and promote your book. In this *Authority Guide*, leading book PR and marketing expert Chantal Cooke, presents 52 tips that will make your book stand out from the crowd, build your credibility as an author, and ensure you achieve those all-important sales.

We hope that you've enjoyed reading this *Authority Guide*. Titles in this series are designed to offer highly practical and easily-accessible advice on a range of business, leadership and management issues.

We're always looking for new authors. If you're an expert in your field and are interested in working with us, we'd be delighted to hear from you. Please contact us at commissioning@suerichardson.co.uk and tell us about your idea for an *Authority Guide*.

EU Safety Representative: euComply OÜ Pärnu mnt 139b-14 11317 Tallinn
Estonia hello@eucompliancepartner.com +33 756 90241

www.ingramcontent.com/pod-product-compliance
Lightning Source LLC
Chambersburg PA
CBHW040521220526
45473CB00013B/2947